# Bollin Valley

## Joan French

*Willow*
PUBLISHING

*Mottram Cross,*

## Willow Publishing 1984
**Willow Cottage, 36 Moss Lane,
Timperley, Altrincham,
Cheshire, WA15 6SZ.**

**ISBN 0 946361 07 X**

Printed by The Commercial
Centre Ltd., Clowes Street,
Hollinwood, Oldham.

**Photography by Keith Warrender**

### Acknowledgements
The author thanks Morris Garratt,
Joan Leach, P Robinson, Project Officer
of the Bollin Valley Project
and Douglas Pickford for their
help in the preparation of this
book.

# Contents

# How it all Began

'Adapted from the book by' – so often you read this when the credits are listed for a film. In my case it was the other way round – let me tell you how it happened. When I retired from a career in Local Government in 1976 I realized that I must extend my interests to ensure that the extra leisure time I would have did not hang heavily. Cine' photography was already a hobby so I pondered whether or not I could make a film on Cheshire villages – after all I lived in one, and it occurred to me that I could go out at any sunny interval – not too far from home and find something of interest.

Then I was lucky – whilst staying with friends I was shown an enchanting film about the river Colne in the Cotswolds and it struck me that the river formed the connecting link for the villages like a necklace on which were strung the pearls. I thought of the river Bollin. Since childhood I had lived within reach of it – it had been our local walking area and an outlet to open country, and so I bought maps and began my research, and eventually the film was finished.

Following the screening of the film for the Old Girls' Society at Altrincham Girls' Grammar School, I was invited to try my hand at writing and this is the result. I hope that as you read on you may find points at which you may join the river and learn something of a different district and of life along its banks.

The meaning and origin of the name of the river is obscure. J. McN. Dodgson in his Place Names of Cheshire points out that the name may come from 'Bolhyn' meaning a torrent or a noisy stream and that eels are found at the eel fare in quite turbulent waters.

It was surprising to find that the river Bollin is approximately thirty miles in length. It rises in the lower reaches of the Pennine Hills above Macclesfield Forest, then proceeds through numerous towns and villages until it joins the Manchester Ship Canal at a place called Bollin Point. The twenty mile length of the valley between Langley in the east to Dunham Park, downstream of Bowdon, make up the Bollin Valley Project area. This began as a three year experiment in 1972 but proved so successful that it has continued. It involves the Countryside Commission and several local authorities who work together with farmers, landowners and local conservation and recreation groups. They all have their own viewpoints but are united in preserving the amenities and the landscape and in providing more opportunities for informal recreation.

Trees have been felled, scrub cleared, pathways renovated and attractive wooden direction signs erected at strategic points to aid the walker. A programme of guided walks of differing distances is published for the summer months and ramblers may join these at various centres. The Bollin Project Officer, whose offices are in Wilmslow, was most helpful in providing me with notes of a survey prepared in his office, and it was on this information that my work began.

It was never my intention to walk every step along the river banks, and indeed there are places where this would be impossible. I intended only to find the chief places of interest through which the river flows and to increase my knowledge of them, and since these proved so numerous to pass on the information to others living nearby. I walked and I motored and all the time I was conscious of the vast numbers living in the North Cheshire area who might also avail themselves of these opportunities and so increase their local history knowledge.

*Styal Woods*

*The Bollin at Bollington, near Dunham Hall.*

Rixton
Old Hall
Warburton
Bollin Point
ALTRINCHAM
Bridgewater
Canal
Dunham Hall
Mill
BOWDON
Heatley
Mill
HALE
Castle
Hill
Ashley
Mill
HALEBARNS
LYMM
Bollington
Lymm Dam
Rostherne Mere
Ashley Hall
Ashley
Cotterill
Clough
Pigley Stairs
Castle Mill
Manchester International
Airport
Styal
Quarry Bank
Mill
The Carrs
WILMSLOW
Wilmslow Park
Adlington Hall
Mottram
Hall
Mottram
Old Hall
Mottram
Cross
Spittle
House
PRESTBURY
Macclesfield
Forest
MACCLESFIELD
Tegg's
Nose
Langley Hall
Langley
Macclesfield
Canal
Sutton
Bollin
Brook

# The Rooftops of Cheshire

Two springs form the source of the river – one on the Tegg's Nose hills, and the other above Macclesfield Forest. On a bitterly cold September day a friend and I motored to the Tegg's Nose Country Park which lies two miles east of Macclesfield and is approached from the A537 Macclesfield to Buxton road.

Tegg's Nose may have been named after an early Norse settler in the area bearing the name of 'Tegge'. An alternative explanation is that the original shape of the hill resembled the head of a young sheep or 'teg'. This is Cheshire's high country – almost like Bronte country in Yorkshire – an open and rocky area full of sheep and heather. If rough walking and winds to blow away the cobwebs are your wish, this is where to go.

The Gritstone Trail passes through the Park. This has been improved and developed by the Countryside and Recreation Division of the Cheshire County Council, and winds its way seventeen miles from Lyme Park in the north (where you can still see a herd of red deer) to Rushton on the Staffordshire border, where it links with the Staffordshire Way and the Mow Cop Trail.

The tough rock is millstone grit which makes excellent building stone. The area was once pitted with quarries, and Tegg's Nose was one of the largest, but it closed in 1955, and seventeen years later the Country Park was created. It is probably more than five hundred years since stone was first removed from here, and a Tegg's Nose stone engraved with a fifteenth century date was found many years ago in Macclesfield. The stone was noted for its pink colour and durability, and was used in restoring some of the Cambridge colleges and to pave many Macclesfield streets.

On another occasion, when I had taken my mother on a car ride above Macclesfield Forest, we discovered the Bollin Brook which drains into Trentabank Reservoir, thence to Ridgegate Reservoir and Bottoms Reservoir east of Langley. In the Forest the North West Water Authority is responsible for the cultivation, felling and stacking of the timber, and we were disappointed not to see the men at work, but interested to see the evidence of their labours.

We motored down to the small village of Langley where Charles Tunnicliffe, R.A., O.B.E., was born in a little two-up and two-down house in 1901. As the son of a shoemaker who later became a farmer, he was to become a leading painter of birds and wild creatures. The Tunnicliffe family later moved to Lane Ends Farm, Sutton Lane Ends, and as a youngster Charles drew the farm animals on the walls of his father's shippen. Later he won a Scholarship to the Royal College of Art in London. His training finished, he was qualified to teach, and this he did in Macclesfield and later at Manchester Grammar School;

*Left: Macclesfield Forest and Shutlingslow from Tegg's Nose Country Park.*
*Below: Tegg's Nose. Its sandy-pink stone has been quarried since the 15th century until 1955.*

but Charles Tunnicliffe wished to devote all his time to his art and to the compilation of a comprehensive encyclopaedia on the study of birds, and in 1947 he and his wife moved to live on the Maltraeth estuary in Anglesey, and from his studio window he had an uninterrupted view of the sea and migratory birds that gathered each year on the Cob. Some friends of mine had a holiday home nearby, where I spent many happy Easter holidays, and through them I was fortunate to meet Charles and Winnie Tunnicliffe.

Bird lovers or those interested in life stories would maybe like to read 'Portrait of a Country Artist' by Ian Niall, the fascinating biography of Charles Tunnicliffe, which includes his lovely bird drawings.

Another place followers of this river should visit is Apprentice Cottage near Sutton Aqueduct. This is the former home of James Brindley, the engineer who consulted with the Duke of Bridgewater and commenced the survey of the Bridgewater Canal (the Worsley to Manchester section). In 1733 he started a seven year apprenticeship as a carpenter and millwright with Abraham Bennett of Sutton, near Macclesfield, and these workshops still remain. He showed an interest in mechanical work and visited nearby mills, and for relaxation he would make model water mills which he set to work in miniature millstreams of his own creation. Brindley engineered the canal system as we know it today, and he was responsible for linking the Trent, Mersey, Thames and Severn.

In 1735 he impressed James Milner of Macclesfield when he helped in the repair of a silk mill damaged by fire. Some of his fellow workmen were scornful of his activities, but at a celebration party on completion of the repairs Milner waged a gallon of ale that 'before this lad's apprenticeship is out he will be a cleverer workman than any here, whether master or man'. Apprentice Cottage is a white building close to the road and a commemorative plaque over the door reads
*'on these premises 1733–1740*
*James Brindley, the famous civil engineer*
*and canal builder served as apprentice*
*to Abraham Bennett.'*

*Stone pillars from Ridge Hall Farm above Sutton. The origins of the pillows is uncertain and they are now in West Park, Macclesfield.*

*The schoolroom, Sutton, where Charles Tunnicliffe was educated.*

*The Queen Anne doorway of 17th century Langley Hall. It was built of stone quarried at Tegg's Nose and was the home of William Smith who introduced silk weaving to the village.*

*The Macclesfield Canal at Sutton.*

*The cottage where James Brindley, engineer to the Duke of Bridgewater, served his apprenticeship.*

9

# Macclesfield~ Silk Town

Macclesfield is a town of hills, steps and cobbled slopes, with alleyways, nooks and crannies in the older district where the silk mills and the weavers' cottages were situated. It enjoys the panorama of the Derbyshire hills, on the crest of which is the Cat and Fiddle, the old inn on the Buxton Road. Many of us in the Hale and Bowdon area are not always pleased to see the hills, since when we do they augur wet weather.

Mentioned in the Domesday Book, the town was formerly part of the demesne of the Saxon Edwin, Earl of Chester. The Norman Earls of Chester were almost royal in precedent and power and they created the forest covering the surrounding hills, which was a favourite hunting ground for the Princes of Wales. A Charter in 1261 granted by Prince Edward, eldest son of Henry III, made the town a free borough with a merchant guild and privileges for the burgesses. An obligation was also imposed and this was to grind at the King's Mill and bake at his oven. Was this a method of imposing taxes, I wonder, or was it an early example of food hygiene and public health regulations?

In 1270 the Manor of Macclesfield was settled on Princess Eleanor, wife of Prince Edward, later to be Edward I, and in 1278 the King and Queen founded the Parochial Chapel of All Saints and All Hallows, now St. Michael's Church. The Market Place, still in regular use, would long ago have been the focal point for social and business activities and the Market Cross is still there, where proclamations were made and from where the yeomen would march to the Battle of Bosworth Field and Flodden Field in 1513.

The present Town Hall was built on the site of the ancient Guildhall, and nearby was the Royal Bakehouse, or the King's Oven mentioned in the original charter where the townspeople were forced to bake their bread. The church stands on high ground and behind were the Gutters – a name given to the town slums. The old Grammar School was also in this area. The hundred and eight steps lead to the lower part of the town, as does Hibel Road once known as Goose Lane down which ducks and geese were driven to the river Bollin below.

Some ladies may still remember wearing blouses or dresses made from Macclesfield silk, but today handloom weavers only produce silk, including squares, handkerchiefs and ties, on a small scale. In 1743 the silk industry really began to flourish here. Charles Roe introduced water-powered machinery to work his button factory in Macclesfield. Others followed, and the silk trade developed rapidly, gaining impetus at the end of the eighteenth century through the arrival of Huguenot weavers.

The Friends of Macclesfield Silk Heritage have devised a trail which follows the streets where the industry flourished, beginning in Duke Street where the industry started. The walk takes in mills, several gentlemen's residences, weavers' cottages and the old school of art. It ends at Macclesfield Sunday School, now recognised by the Department of the Environment as a building of national importance, and to be used as a Heritage Centre to show the town's history and principal industries. A pamphlet giving details of the walk can be obtained from the Town Hall.

The river is culverted in part of Macclesfield, but unfortunately it runs through the Hurdsfield Estate where I was sad to see the banks in use as a car breaker's yard. From here it runs on through open country towards Prestbury.

*Left: The Town Hall, built in 1823, stands on the site of 'King's Oven' where the town's bread used to be baked. Below left: Glacial boulder, West Park, Macclesfield. Below right: Macclesfield Heritage Centre.*

*Above:*
*The hundred and eight steps leading up to the highest part of Macclesfield.*

*Right:*
*Hand loom weavers in 1933 at Paradise Mill, Macclesfield. The mill on Park Lane is now a working silk museum with many of the looms in their original setting.*

*Norman doorway incorporated into the chapel at the side of St. Peter's Church, Prestbury.*

# Prestbury~ Priests' Town

Whether one travels North or South in this country it always interests me to note the different characteristics of each county. You can instinctively tell when you leave the smooth plains of Cheshire and move into the bleaker hills and moors of Derbyshire, or into the more rolling country of Shropshire with its red bricked farmsteads, or again into the rich red loam fields of the Cotswolds with their delightful villages of honey golden stone cottages.

As you travel you often find one unique village which pleases and which remains in the memory. I am thinking of places like Lavenham and Cavendish in Suffolk, Broadway in Gloucestershire, Rye in Sussex. Such a place is Prestbury. It is prestigious, wealthy and of all the Cheshire villages is one of the greatest beauty, which attracts without need of commercial gimmicks. Of the seventy villages which compete in the Best Kept Village competition annually, it is inevitably first or second and proudly displays its appropriate sign.

Prestbury is a long and narrow parish situated on the Bollin and extending along its valley through dairy farming country towards Wilmslow. It is a neat and tidy place. During a leisurely stroll through the village one can see old timber buildings, several old inns, a church built of stone from nearby Kerridge and some interesting shops.

The name Prestbury means Priests' town (from the Saxon Preostburgh) and historians agree that it was here that the first community of missionary priests settled to preach the Gospel. It is believed that there was a church here long before William the Conqueror. In about 1841 work was carried out on the chancel and fragments of a Saxon cross were found, dated about the 8th Century. This is now in a display cabinet at the rear of the church and close to a small building known as the Norman Chapel, which was probably built on the site of the old Saxon edifice. The chapel has a beautiful doorway worth admiring.

It is thought that the cross was placed in position by early Saxon converts to Christianity to commemorate the spot where the Gospel was first preached in the locality; the river would be easily available for the baptisms. At one time natives of the Parish enjoyed special privileges at Brazennose College, Oxford, owing to the fact that Sir Richard Sutton, a founder of the college, was born at Sutton Old Hall, Macclesfield which was within the Parish. The present church was probably built about 1220, and the first record of its having a vicar is 1230.

*Left: The 14th century Priest's House. Above: The main street looking towards Ford House.*

In 1850 the settlement consisted of three hundred and seventy persons, with a main street and Pearl Street across the river. Later a bridge was built near the present Bridge Inn. In the latter part of the 19th century the population fell as agricultural workers migrated to the urban areas. Later this was reversed and by 1931 the population had grown to over three hundred and seventy. Now with the village within easy reach of Manchester Airport, and with good rail and road services into Manchester, only a small number are agricultural workers and more than half commute more than ten miles to their place of work.

The Prestbury Amenity Society has published an attractive leaflet listing and detailing twenty-four buildings of interest in the village. This may be obtained from Ford House, the black and white 17th century house near the bridge and opposite the Hotel is now used as a social centre for the parish, but for a time in the 19th century it was the Roebuck Public House.

One October my cousin and I followed the Village Walk. As directed we set off from the white mansion known as Prestbury Hall, which lies at the top of the village street. Dr. Hope, an early Professor of Medicine at University College, London, once lived there, and during the Second World War part of St. Mary's Maternity

Hospital, in Manchester, was evacuated there.

Next to the Hall is a bank. This building was erected in 1720 and was originally the village school which was endowed with £10 for the purpose of teaching ten of the village's poorest children. Wherever you see long horizontal windows in the upper storey of old houses or cottages you may assume that weaving took place, since these gave maximum light for the use of the looms. An attractive cottage with mullioned windows opposite the bank was so used, and there were many other weavers' cottages in the village, notably Brooks Cottages in Pearl Street, and Spindles' terrace in the High Street. Hall Farm was once at this end of the village, and on the site of Royle's Garage were the outbuildings and piggeries. There were in fact several farms in the village street.

The Legh Arms probably dates from 1500. Originally it was the Saracen's Head and known locally as The Black Boy. Parish tea parties were once held in a room over the stables and on Fair days the local inhabitants gathered there. Prestbury was famous for its cattle fairs, held annually in the street on April 28th and October 10th; the last one was held just before the outbreak of the 1914–18 War.

15

*Above: Prestbury. Below: Mottram Old Hall, built in the mid 15th century, surrounded by a wide moat. In 1728 the estate covered more than 500 acres with orchards, a dove house and a corn mill.*

*Spittle House stands on the site of two hospitals for itinerant lepers who were barred from the towns. The cruck barn built between 1350 and 1400 is all that remains of the original hospital.*

Swanwick House stands almost opposite the church. This is an imposing three-storied house, and was named after the owner of the mill in Bollin Grove. Opposite the lychgate stands the former vicarage, known as the Priest's House where marriage ceremonies took place. It is now a bank – a most attractive timber framed building with stone slate roof.

Beyond Ford House the river is crossed by a wooden bridge completed in 1979. Bollin Grove follows the river between rows of workers' cottages to the site of the Butley Manor Corn Mill in use in the 17th century as a Manorial mill, later becoming a cotton mill and then a silk weaving mill. Spittal House, the oldest building in the area, lies a quarter of a mile downstream. It was once two 'cruck' buildings built by the monks of St. Werburgh about 1350, and one of the buildings is thought to have been used as a leper hospital.

Near the bridge, turning into Bollin Grove I noticed that the river bed is 'laid' with stone flags and I wondered whether this was part of the ford by which the water was formerly crossed at the end of Pearl Street. The street may have got its name from a pearl meaning a bubble (those in the water arising from the ford) or alternatively from Pearlina, a hand twist of silk and wool used for knitting. In the 1900's it was called Pell Street after the name 'pel' given to silk yarn. Butley Hall, where bear baiting bouts were held in the 19th century, lies in the trees at the end of the car park.

There has been a Mill for 700 or 800 years on Prestbury Meadow, and behind the Bridge Hotel the present Hamlyn Mill replaced one burnt down in 1940. The Bridge Hotel was originally cottages dating from 1626. In spite of the transformation the old appearance has been preserved and in the lounge some of the daub and wattle has been retained along with the old beams.

Standing on the bridge you realize that the river divides the village into two parts – the higher section where the Hall, Church and main shops lie and the lower part with the row of shops and cottages on one side of the road ending with the public car park. The river clings to the side of Bollin Grove, encloses three sides of the school premises and then proceeds past Spittle House, the sewage works with its settling tanks, through open country past Mottram Woods, Mottram Hall Hotel and Mottram Old Hall.

Before continuing to Wilmslow visitors may wish to turn aside to see Adlington Hall, once the site of a Saxon hunting lodge. This is an historic and lovely building combining architecture of the 15th, 16th and 18th centuries, part brick and part timber. For over six centuries it has been the home of the Leghs. The lodge was built between two huge oak trees which still have their roots in the ground and support one end of the Great Hall, which contains an organ installed about 1680 and once played upon by Handel. The hall is open to the public and recitals are occasionally given.

# Wilmslow

One of the most attractive places to visit in North East Cheshire is Wilmslow. It lies in the valleys of the Rivers Bollin and Dean. It is a pleasant residential area surrounded on all but the north side by open country, and is a popular commuter area for those working in Manchester or Stockport. The town has been developed in keeping with its pleasant aspect and large stores and a theatre have increased the amenities.

At the rear of the Rex Theatre you will find Romany's caravan. 'Out with Romany' was a natural history programme on the BBC Northern Children's Hour just after the last War. Romany was played by the Rev. Bramwell Evans.

Wilmslow is not mentioned in the Domesday Book nor is there any record of le Bolyn, the name by which this part was known, and it is probable that the river gained its name from this source. There are two theories of the origin of the name Wilmslow. One is that it was named after the burial ground of the first William le Bolyn, known as William's lowe – and the second is that the church of St. Bartholomew was built on rising ground overlooking the crossing point of the river, and the rise was called William's Hill – later to become Wilmslow.

Travelling from Prestbury towards Wilmslow on the A538 the river flows for about one-and-a-half miles to our right and enters the district through Wilmslow Park and under the railway viaduct.

To the south side of the valley was once Bollin Hall, demolished in 1842 to make way for these bridges. The house probably dated back to the medieval estate of the Fittons and according to legend may have been the birthplace of Ann Boleyn.

The portion of the Park nearest to the site of the old hall is now in the ownership of the North West Water Board, and the river, now fifteen to eighteen feet in width, flows through landscaped grounds past offices and sewage treatment works. The river passes under the busy A34 road leading to Handforth, Cheadle and Manchester and flows past the Memorial Gardens, facing a row of cottages, which may well have been weavers' cottages, since they are in Mill Lane.

The church of St. Bartholomew lies to the left in Chancel Lane, and is first mentioned in 1264. It was built for Sir Richard Fitton of Bollin. The present church, where Gladstone worshipped as a boy, largely dates from 1517–37, when it was rebuilt by the rector Henry Trafford. It has seven bells cast in 1733, and there was once a saying that the Wilmslow bells ring themselves since a family called Bell were the bellringers. The roof of the church contains much of the original sixteenth century woodwork.

*The oak lychgate at the entrance to St. Bartholomew's Churchyard was built in 1904.*

*By the main church porch there is a 16th century gravestone for the children belonging to one of the ministers.*

*Romany's caravan.*

*Pownall Hall Bridge*

From the graveyard at the rear of the church the river can be seen flowing through the Carrs, formerly pasture land used by the villagers on which to graze their cattle, and which was purchased by the former Wilmslow UDC in 1935 for use as a public open space. 'The Boddington Playing Fields' were given in 1925 by a member of the brewery family who once lived at Pownall Hall. Together they form a fifty acre riverside park linking Wilmslow with Styal Country Park and includes pitch and putt, tennis courts, bowling green and children's play park. There is a one-and-a-half mile circular walk through woodlands past a ruined chapel, the walk commencing at the car park in Chancel Lane. The word 'Carrs' is derived from the Norse word 'Kjarr' which means 'meadow recovered from bog'.

In this area there were cotton and silk mills and remains of the latter can still be seen. Styal Road runs alongside the Carrs, and at the foot of the hill approaching Styal is a bridge called Twinney's Bridge, which stands where the rivers Dean and Bollin join.

A second car park adjoins the bridge and from here, should you wish, you may explore and find the Pownall Chapel. It is in the woods to your right as you walk back towards Wilmslow. Cross the bridge over the river, turn left, and then keeping to the right of the fields, walk through the woods. The trees grow on a steeply rising slope, on the top of which can be seen the rear of the modern houses built in Pownall Park. Having walked three to four hundred yards you will notice on your path heaps of large stones scattered around – on one of which I read the words 'Chapelle of Saint ..........'. These are part of the

remains of the Chapel. At this point climb up the slope to a path running along the top and you will find further remains. The Chapel was built in 1888 for Mr. Henry Boddington, of nearby Pownall Hall, using stone from St. Bartholomew's Church. The ruins lie next to the Commemoration Oak Tree.

Until the 1940's the building was in good repair – then wartime industry required all the iron and steel available and the protective iron railings were removed, and vandals and general misuse did the rest. The chapel was demolished in the late 1940's. Vandals pushed some of the stones down the slope. A local school had plans to remove some of the carved stones and partially rebuild the chapel but because of lack of funds the idea was abandoned.

The lower three to four feet of the chapel walls remain and the shape of the building can be seen. Modifications to the original old stone walls have been made, using red brick to line the inner walls, and a tiled floor and concrete altar step have been added more recently.

Returning to the car park you may, by crossing a small wooden footbridge, continue into Styal Woods. Be sure to keep to the right-hand side path otherwise you may get lost behind the I.C.I. Research building on the Wilmslow/ Altrincham Road. If travelling by car along Styal Road you will eventually pass H.M. Prison, which is for the custody and reformation of women prisoners. The village of Styal is now very near and as you enter you pass on your left the entrance to Styal Country Park and the National Trust property, Quarry Bank Mill and estate.

*The Carrs*

*Right: Styal Woods*

# Styal

It is comparatively easy to reach Styal from a wide area; it is a compact and attractive village of black and white Cheshire buildings and has one of the National Trust's most interesting properties – Quarry Bank Mill. The mill, along with the village farms and woodland were given to the National Trust in 1939; the mill itself was closed in 1959.

The mill was built in 1784 by Samuel Greg, and is one of the best preserved rural factory colonies of the period. The site was chosen because of the fourteen foot fall of water at this point on the Bollin, since it was intended that the cotton spinning mill should be powered from the river. Power loom weaving was introduced in 1835. From 1904 water driven turbines were used instead of the water wheel. Following a special appeal for funds, made by the Trust, a water wheel will be in use again in the near future. Greg had a vision of fine mill building set in the wooded valley of the river Bollin, and of well-housed, healthy, educated workers. He had his critics however, and Engels, whose account of working class conditions in the early 19th century was to fire Karl Marx, saw the mill as a more subtle but still pernicious form of exploitation.

The village school was built in 1822 and all apprentices had to attend. The school is still used today. Oak Cottages were built in 1822 to house families of mill workers following a period of great expansion at the mill, and a bell was rung to summon them all to work.

Samuel Greg converted many farm buildings to house his people. Shaw's Fold is an example of a timbered barn enlarged by an extra storey. It was the wish of the Greg family that the mill and the village should be preserved as monuments of their period. This has been amply fulfilled since the mill is now busy and working again and the village a memorial to their lives.

The Quarry Bank Mill Trust Ltd. was formed in 1978 and David Sekers, a member of the family who came from Hungary to found a silk industry in Cumbria, was engaged as Museum Director. He initiated Styal Workshop, now recognised as a centre for art students and craftsmen. He felt that the processes of spinning and weaving were difficult to study by reading alone and could be more readily followed by watching skilled people at work. It is far more interesting for visitors to the mill to see spinning demonstrations and hand and power loom weaving – but for even greater enthusiasm and interest, participation should be the goal.

*Above: Styal Cross*

A long room, formerly used as a weaving shed, was converted, and equipped to become the Workshop. An Education Officer was engaged and now school parties may book time for practical work in spinning, weaving, printing and dyeing. Peter Collingwood and John Hinchcliffe need no introduction to weavers and connoisseurs of modern textiles and they are just two lecturers of the two-to-six day courses.

Readers may recall having seen the television documentary, 'The Craft of the Weaver', so clearly and pleasantly presented by Ann Sutton. She visited the mill to lecture to members of several Weavers' Guilds during the winter of 1982. As a close relative I went, accompanied by a party of friends, and we were delighted to see the enthusiasm shown by a packed audience.

Visitors to Styal could happily spend a day there ambling through the village; perhaps calling for a snack at the Old Ship Inn before visiting the mill and the attractive Mill Shop. The walks by the river and through the woods are pleasant throughout the year. I remember one day visiting during the winter, accompanied by two young friends, who were thrilled to find long icicles hanging from the rocks in grotto-like enclosures on our way. They snapped these off intending to take them home to show their parents. 'Perhaps we could put them in your fridge until we leave,' they said. Alas they were disappointed!

Styal is situated about ten miles south of Manchester, four miles from the M56 junction 6, and two and a half miles from Wilmslow off the B5166. There is also a frequent train service to Styal from Manchester Piccadilly. Free parking and picnic areas are available and light refreshments can be purchased in the Mill Kitchen throughout the year.

*Below: Oak Cottages*

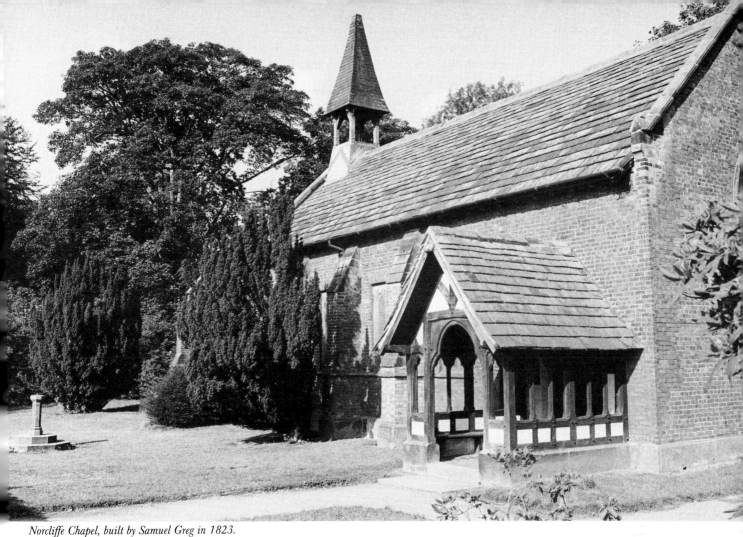

*Norcliffe Chapel, built by Samuel Greg in 1823.*

*The weir for the mill pool which was in use until 1959.*

*Samuel Greg opened Styal Shop then later it was managed by mill employees.*

*Castle Mill as it was.*

# Homeground~ Ringway, Hale Barns & Hale

*Castle Mill*

*e now demolished Ashley Mill.*

Leaving Styal, the model village which fulfilled the aspirations of Samuel Greg, it is well worth travelling around the perimeter of the Manchester International Airport, situated in the old Parish of Ringway, and where several of the old farms still exist, for example Davenport Green Hall Farm dated 1617 and recently renovated. Ringway Chapel (no longer used) goes back to the days when the Church of England was part of the Church of Rome. The name of Ringway is synonymous with Manchester Airport. The City of Manchester was the first British municipality to establish an airport. During the Second World War it was used for the training of paratroopers.

Along the road from Styal to our next place of call there is a vantage point for 'plane spotters'. The road joins the A538 at a point adjacent to the Valley Lodge Hotel, a chalet-type building reminiscent of Switzerland or Austria. Near here the main runway of the airport has recently been extended in order to cope with the growing traffic of the second largest airport in Europe, and this necessitated a portion of the river being diverted.

It was here in the fields below the road bridge one Sunday morning that I came across a local club of canoeists (just one of many activities which take place on the waterway). I had heard that they were to start a voyage from this point along the river for ten miles to the weir at Bollington. My friend and I watched about 20 canoes set off, then we followed by car along the road taking the left turn to Ashley skirting Cotterill Clough and Castle Mill until we reached Ashley Heath. Here we parked the car, set off over the fields to a viaduct under which the water was in full spate and the canoeists were 'shooting the rapids'. We were unable to follow the whole course, which was to take about four hours, so we returned home after reaching Ashley Mill House.

Castle Mill was built in 1808, but in May 1872 a reservoir near Macclesfield burst and devastated the Bollin Valley. The weir was washed away and Ashley Mill was also damaged and put out of use. Only Ashley Mill House now remains, though the site of the old mill can be identified. In the 1930's an open air swimming pool known as Castle Mill Lido was built opposite the mill, but this fell out of favour in due course and was replaced by a private house. When Castle Mill was demolished in 1954 a house was also built on these foundations.

Cotterill Clough Nature Reserve lies between Sunbank Lane, Hale Barns and the Castle Mill Road to Ashley. In Cotterill Clough there is a large boulder with a copper plaque with the words inscribed:
*'In Memory of Thomas Alfred Coward, M.Sc. 1867–1933, Cotterill Clough and Marbury Reed Bed were purchased by public subscription to remain forever undisturbed Nature Reserves as a memorial to his great services to natural science'.*

*Hale Barns Unitarian Chapel*

*Hale*

*Pigley Stair Bridge.*

The Clough is a preserved sanctuary for wild life and the plants growing there, but individuals and interested parties, such as natural history societies etc. are allowed to visit by permit as long as they observe the rules that no specimens may be removed without written authority from the Cheshire Conservation Trust Ltd.

Leaving Cotterill Clough and crossing the stile near Castle Mill you may walk along the river which is now possibly twelve to twenty feet wide, and here, below Pigley Stairs, is an area enjoyed very much by children in the summer — swimming, paddling and having picnics. Beside the wooden bridge several signposts lead to other parts of the valley – Mill Lane, Ross Mill or Sunbank Lane. Following the route to Ross Mill you may continue past 'Wolff's Farm' and on to Hale Golf Course. This 9-hole course may also be approached from Rappax Road, Hale, one of the luxury areas of our district. It gives lovely views over the river and several greens and fairways run alongside the water, which must add to the relaxation of the many players. There is an abundance of entrances to the river in this district – these may be found from Chapel Lane, Ross Mill Lane, Bankhall Lane and Ashley Heath, from whence you may travel along towards Bowdon and Bowdon Vale. If you decide to leave the river below Grange Road, Bowdon you will notice on the house numbered 10 a blue plaque telling you that Mr. T. A. Coward, the Naturalist, once lived there.

In my eagerness to tell you of the canoeing activities on the river and of the delights of Cotterill Clough, I strayed from the Wilmslow, Altrincham road. Had I not done so you might have continued towards Hale Barns.

The name 'Halh' was Saxon for nook or shelter, and Hale Barns was once noted for its old tithe barn. I remember the place when it was a small village with very few shops, but it has developed into a thriving community.

In Chapel Lane there is a picturesque Unitarian Chapel built in 1723 as the Presbyterian Meeting House, and surrounded by a small churchyard. Inside there are box pews grouped round the pulpit with its sounding board. In the village is also the Unitarian School built in 1740.

Hale is a most attractive small town which has retained its character in spite of controlled development. Opposite the bowling green on the corner of Legh Road is an old cottage building dating back to 1406, and once called Ollerbarrow Farm. After the First World War, plans were drawn up for this site to be used as a cinema, but owing to public pressure these were withdrawn. In the Second War it was used by the Women's Voluntary Services, and later as a small Police Station. In 1981 it became a listed building, and now having been restored it is used by a building society. At the far end of the town, on the way to Bowdon, the station has also been listed. Note the old drinking fountain in front of the station buildings.

*Above: Altrincham Station clock, Stamford New Road. Below: Altrincham Market.*

*Goose Green*

# Altrincham to Tatton

At the beginning I said that I was only going to write of those places which edged on to the river, but one road leads to another and you are enticed to follow, so I shall describe a few places which you may visit in the area.

The river Bollin does not touch the old market town of Altrincham, but because it is a good centre I will write of it and some of the interesting places nearby.

Altrincham was probably founded in the 8th century by a Saxon settler called Tring, who pitched camp and lit his fires in an enclosure which is now the Old Market Place. A Charter granted by Edward I gave permission for the holding of a Tuesday Market and now the market is also open on Fridays and Saturdays. The Court Leet, the forerunner of local government, had many and varied powers – it regulated the conduct of the markets and fairs and its constables preserved the public peace. As well as constables there were market lookers, chimney lookers, dog muzzlers and ale tasters. The Charter awarded a Fair which was replaced in 1319 by the 'Sanjam' (St. James') Fair, held regularly until 1895.

Thomas de Quincey visited Altrincham in 1802 and again in 1816 and wrote of the gaiety of the scene as he looked down on the Market Place from the window of the Inn where he stayed, on to the stalls bright with fruit and vegetables, and of the attractiveness of the bonny village girls.

During the 1745 Rebellion, Bonnie Prince Charlie's troops gathered in the Old Market Place and demanded lodgings. One trooper seeing a man in Well Lane (Victoria Street) wearing a pair of new boots shouted 'Hoot mon, we mun ha' your brogues'. Many stories are told of this historic spot, such as the man who in 1809 offered his wife for sale and found a buyer for 18 pence!!

The Bridgewater Canal and then the South Junction and Altrincham railway brought commercial prosperity to the town and it became the centre of the machine tool industry and of market gardening. Redevelopment of the town has transformed it from a medium sized old market town to one of large stores, car parks, banks and office blocks – but you can still feel the atmosphere of the more gentle days in the Old Market Place (which no longer holds the market), in Goose Green and on the Downs. At the station you will notice the clock tower built in 1880.

Goose Green is a quaint corner of the old town, and is just off the main street. Underneath a recently erected piece of sculpture by Sean Compton of Two Geese, you will find information on the history of the area. In the 18th and 19th centuries the locality was known as Pinfold Brow and Goose Green and there was a wheelwright's shop and a

*Lychgate at Rostherne Church. It was built in 1640 and is one of the oldest gates in Cheshire.*

forge; handloom weavers and market gardeners lived locally. At Hale Moss nearby, there was grazing for cattle, horses and donkeys, ducks and geese. Each September as part of Bowdon Wakes, sports and a fair were held with itinerant shows, roundabouts, swing boats and gingerbread stalls.

The Downs will lead you on towards Bowdon, but climbing upwards you will be attracted by the well-maintained terrace of Georgian houses.

The village of Ashley lies in the southern outskirts of Altrincham. Ashley Hall was once the home of the Breretons, the last being Sir William Brereton, one of Cromwell's Commanders. There was said to be one of King John's hunting lodges on the site but the present house is of a later period. It passed in the 19th century to the Egertons of Tatton and they built the village school and the red brick church of St. Elizabeth, dated 1880. The Greyhound is a popular meeting place and Inn.

Just off the Chester Road outside Altrincham is Rostherne Mere which is Cheshire's largest lake covering 115 acres. It is a bird sanctuary and lies close to the church in this pretty village on the north side of Tatton Park. The church is 12th century and has been well restored.

In Cicely Mill Lane are two 17th century cottages, while at the southern end of the village is St. Mary's Square, a small residential estate built in 1910 for workers in Tatton Park.

Don't look for a village at Tatton – there isn't one. The parish consists only of the 1000 acre estate of the late Lord Egerton, now a National Trust property of immense popularity. It began as a small homestead cleared from the forest by an Anglo-Saxon farmer called Tata. The Egertons

were masters here for 380 years, but apart from Sir Thomas Egerton, adviser to Elizabeth I, produced no other national figures. They were, however, influential in Cheshire, their wealth coming from investments in factories. They had great social conscience and helped the community. In 1887 the Prince and Princess of Wales stayed here when opening the Royal Jubilee Exhibition in Manchester, and to commemorate the visit the Prince planted a tree which still thrives near the Orangery.

The 4th and last Baron Egerton (1874–1958) had many interests; he was a pioneer in motor cars and an aviator, and had his own wireless transmitting station at Tatton. He was also a much travelled big game hunter and divided his time between Tatton and his Kenya estate, where he fostered native industry. It was he who planted the large collection of rhododendrons, azaleas and rare shrubs at Tatton, and provided the Boys' Club at Knutsford.

The deer park and 19th century house provide immense interest, the house containing collections of pictures, furniture, silver and china. The garden of 50 acres includes a Japanese garden and Shinto temple. Tatton Mere supports many species of wildfowl and sailing facilities. Various cultural activities take place in the house including concerts and exhibitions, and the County Show takes place here annually.

Knutsford has two claims to fame. It is reputed to have been the place where King Canute (Knut) forded a lily stream dividing Over Knutsford from Nether Knutsford – and, what is more certain, it was the background for Mrs. Gaskell's work 'Cranford'.

It is a pleasant residential town and tourist centre. There are two parallel streets – an upper and the older lower – with another running in a line with the Northwich Road, which has several Georgian houses, separated from it by an expanse of heath. The thirty-six acres of heath are now recognised as Common Land and were formerly the venue of Knutsford Races for two hundred years until 1873. Now they are used each year for May Day celebrations when a vivid procession passes through the streets, culminating in the crowning of the May Queen.

Knutsford was a prosperous market town in the seventeenth century and the old centre is still a busy shopping area and retains the air of a Georgian country town. during the Festival of Britain in 1951, a number of commemorative plaques were provided to indicate well-known sites and buildings:

*The Sessions House* was designed by Thomas Harrison, built in the renaissance style and completed in 1818. Quarter Sessions were held here from January 1575 to December 1971, when they were replaced by the County Court under the Courts Act, 1971. At *Brook Street Unitarian Chapel*, (1689) Mrs. Gaskell worshipped and taught in the Sunday School. She, her husband and her ancestors are buried in the chapel yard. *The Lord Eldon Inn* was the birthplace of the first Knutsford May Queen crowned in 1864 – Miss Sarah Ann Pollitt. *Heathwaite, 17 Gaskell Avenue* was the childhood home of Mrs. Gaskell. *Trumpet Major Smith*, who sounded the charge at Balaclava, lived in a house in Freeholder's Terrace, Stanley Road. *The Parish Church* (1744) is early Georgian but registers go back to 1581. The brass lectern was made out of shell cases, originally the property of Toc H. 'Tubby' Clayton, founder of Toc H, who stayed in Knutsford. The unique style of Richard Harding Watt can be seen in Drury Lane, Legh Road and King Street. He was influenced by architecture observed during travels on the continent.

*Rostherne Mere, from the Church.*

*Part of an eastern-style laundry built in the early years of this century in Drury Lane, Knutsford.*

*The Gaskell Memorial Tower, built by Richard Harding Watt in 1907.*

# Bowdon

From Hale Barns, Hale Golf Course and Ashley Heath, the river runs through agricultural land under and alongside the M56 motorway, which in recent years has helped so many in this area to gain a quick retreat from Greater Manchester to Chester and North Wales.

Two footpaths from the river will lead you to Bowdon or Bowdon Vale. One is past Grange Farm and up Grange Road to Langham Road. The other leads past The Priory and into Priory Road. The main portion of the house is Georgian. It stands in a mysterious position since from the pathway at the rear (which links Bowdon Vale with the Bollin and Rostherne) you view it through thick shrubbery and a net of boughs and twigs. In the garden is an old milestone, and in crumbled Roman lettering it gives the distances from Altrincham and Manchester to the north, and from Knutsford, Northwich and Chester to the south. I fear 'The Priory' is a misnomer, since it is doubtful if it ever was, though ecclesiastical records show that it was once Bowdon Vicarage, and even to this day the road from Priory Road through Bowdon Vale Village is named Vicarage Lane.

The Romans passed through Bowdon, and the (Chester Road/Dunham Road) was part of Watling Street. The part relating to this region commenced at the ford of Mersey (Stretford), entered Broadheath through a cutting of the Bridgewater Canal and the enclosures of Oldfield Hall, crossed the Moss, ascended the Hill at Street Head Cottages, skirted Dunham Park and then joined the modern road at Newbridge Hollow. Further evidence of Roman occupation in this area is indicated by the Tumuli or Barrows (Burial Mounds) in Baguley, Bollington and Dunham Park.

Bowdon is indeed of ancient origin – it is known that a church existed before the Norman Conquest; a silver penny from the reign of Eadmund, a Saxon king, was unearthed in the churchyard. According to the Domesday Book there was a church here at the time of William the Conqueror, and there are traces of three later churches dated 1100, 1320 and 1510. The present church built probably between 1856 and 1860, and dominated by a tower of over 90 feet, is conspicuous from afar, since it stands up on a hill. Church Registers began in 1628.

The church houses numerous interesting relics, as well as containing notable stained glass windows. The tomb of Sir William Baguley, who was known to have lived at Baguley Old Hall in 1319, was found in a garden in Partington. It was moved to the precincts of Baguley Old Hall and later to Bowdon Church. The effigy is depicted as dressed in chain mail.

There was once a custom which was almost universal throughout the country – the ceremony of electing Boy Bishops. This was observed by parishes, cathedrals, monasteries, private and domestic chapels in the great houses. The election took place on St. Nicholas Day (6th December) and the encumbents held office until Holy Innocents' Day (28th December). In the event of such a boy dying during his term of office, he was buried with due solemnity as if a real bishop, and a monument was provided. Obviously this rarely happened since the period covered only twenty-two days. There is one of these monuments in Salisbury Cathedral (38½ inches in length) and another in Bowdon Church (this one is between 32 and 33 inches high). The Bowdon boy is supposedly dated

*The Bollin at Watlingford, Bowdon, where there was reputed to have been a skirmish between the forces of Henry the Second. In the background is the small motte and bailey castle of Watch Hill which guarded the river crossing.*

about 1150 A.D. and the inscription reads 'Misere Mei dens' (Have mercy on me, O God). The custom was abolished in the reign of Henry VIII. Orders to be observed by the bell ringers signed by ten Wardens and ringers once read:

*'You ringers all observe these orders well*
*He pays his 6d. that o'erturns the bell*
*And he that rings with either spurs or hat*
*Must pay his 6d. certainly for that.*
*And he that rings and does disturb a peal*
*Must pay his 6d. or a gun of ale.*
*These laws elsewhere in every church are used*
*That bells and ringers may not be abused'.*

In the churchyard are two or three yew trees, one of which is reputedly 800 years old. They are relics of Saxon christianity. The road which leads to the church, The Firs, was once known as Burying Lane.

John Wesley is known to have visited the Chapel at Bowdon in 1790 and is one of the first churches mentioned in his Journal, but the Dome Chapel subsequently built to replace it, no longer exists. The church became too costly to run and the last service was in 1966.

For many years Bowdon Wakes Races were held during the last days of September, and since houses named Racefield and Racehill are situated on Dunham Road, one wonders if this is where they took place. Prizes varied from silver cups for horse racing, to legs of mutton for those who brought the mutton down from the top of a greasy pole. Jockeys were ordered to attend with 'clean faces, and not only must the hair be well-combed down, but the manes and tails of their donkeys likewise in order to keep up a dignity befitting the important event'. One wonders if these events were the forerunner to the Altrincham Agricultural Show once recognised as 'the largest one-day show in England' and held annually on the Devisdale in Bowdon.

In the age of cock fighting and bull baiting, these occurred in the ring which lay between Bowdon Church and the Griffin Hotel, until the Vicar of Bowdon abolished them in 1815.

*Left: The stables were built in 1721. Above: The weir by Bollington Mill.*

# Dunham Massey

Again the river meanders through fields and under Watling Street, the old Roman road. It then flows through water meadows to approach Dunham Massey and the Park, part of the estate of Dunham Massey Hall, home of the Earls of Stamford and Warrington.

Let us leave the river for a while to visit this lovely old house with its antique furniture, priceless paintings and precious Huguenot silver. To do so, if travelling by road, we would turn into Charcoal Road where there are the former homes of the cotton barons. Many have been converted into flats or, a practise becoming more common, houses have been demolished and modern homes erected amidst the old gardens. In the gardens of one house adjacent to the first Park, are planted thousands of daffodils, to which people make annual pilgrimages each Spring.

Opposite the first lodge to the Hall there is a large, deep pit. This was used as a hearth for burning wood to charcoal – the heating power of which is more than twice that of untreated wood and burns without smoke or fumes. It was therefore largely used as a fuel in the reduction of metallic oxides such as iron and lead; the salt and glaze industries also used large quantities. It was charcoal burning that was partially responsible for the destruction of England's woods during the late middle ages.

The first mention of habitation at Dunham Massey is of a castle, in existence in 1323, being defended by its owner, Hamon de Massey, against Henry II. The families who have lived at Dunham Hall have been six Masseys, six Booths and six Greys, and the present house was built in 1732 for George Booth.

In 1976 the house and estate were bequeathed to the National Trust under the Will of Roger Grey, the 10th Earl of Stamford. In the closed season, concerts take place in the Great Gallery, and craft fairs are regularly held adjoining the shop and restaurant.

In the Park is a herd of 300 fallow deer – rather less than in 1844 when there were 500. They are very tame but visitors are requested not to feed them since they could easily knock over youngsters. In the Smithy pool you can watch herons, Canada geese, mallards, coots and tufted ducks.

Continuing from the pool and past the Hall and stables you will come to the water mill. It was built in 1616 in Elizabethan style with multi-gables and mullion windows. It is all that remains of the complex built by Sir George Booth, the first baronet. Originally a corn mill, it was refitted as a saw mill around 1860, but became disused about 1895. Restored by the Trust, its new overshot wheel drives, by means of line shafting, the machinery restored to working order after over eighty years' dereliction.

Go on down the path and over the stile and you will arrive at Bollington corn mill. It is a five-storied building in the style of the late 18th century. The Bollin had a weir built across it and a mill race led from above the weir to the mill, which has since been used as a refrigerated cheese store and is now storing garden fertilizers. From this point you may look back across the weir and the water meadows towards the Chester Road, or forward and see that the river runs under a bridge, over which flows the Bridgewater Canal. Both the river and canal are enjoyed on fine days by fishermen, canoeists and private motor boats.

Before leaving this particular reach of the river you may wish to visit one of the attractive old inns – The Swan with Two Necks at Bollington, or The Vine at Dunham Woodhouses. Your preference may be for a ramble, and a pleasant walk around Dunham is to turn left out of the National Trust Car Park, climb on to the canal bank and continue until you reach one of the bridges in sight of Dunham Village. You will pass the old Church of St. Marks where you will be able to see the graves of the 9th Countess of Stamford and her son, the 10th Earl. Continue down the road past the entrance to the Axe and Cleaver Inn, the Post Office and the big tree and return to the Hall and the car park.

Bollington Corn Mill

*Right: The water mill.*

# Warburton, Heatley & Bollin Point

After the unusual view of a river travelling under a canal, the next few miles of its course are commonplace. It runs through sewage beds and market gardens towards Heatley Flour Mill.

Turning left out of the Dunham Hall new car park I went under the narrow canal bridge and motored towards Dunham Woodhouses. It is only a small hamlet but its black and white cottages and the old Vine Inn are attractive and typical of Cheshire buildings. This is a market gardening area and many of the farmsteads advertise their produce for sale. I continued into Warburton – a small hamlet astride the road to Heatley and Lymm. It derived its name from Saint Werburgh, daughter of King Wulfere of Mercia. In the Domesday Book the quaint church is named as 'Warburgetone', so there was a place of worship there before the Norman conquest, and also a Priory. A second church was built in 1885 by R. E. Egerton Warburton and this is still in regular use. Five of the thirty-three known rectors were called Warburton and indeed the Hall, which was on the east side of the church and village and which no longer exists, housed this family from the end of the 13th century.

A directory of Cheshire for 1850 stated that inhabitants of Warburton were exempt from serving on juries and not liable to tolls at any fairs or markets in the county – but today Warburton is the only place in the area where travellers have to pay a toll to cross the Manchester Ship Canal into Lancashire.

In the 19th century, when residents of local parishes established friendly societies and burial clubs to care for the sick and bereaved, Warburton originated a 'Cow Club' – its object being to provide benefits for members whose cows fell sick or died!

The Saracens Head at Warburton is a popular hostelry where there is a weekly flea market.

On past Warburton Church, I again crossed over the river and by the bridge saw Heatley Flour Mill on my left. The original mill stood on the site of the bridge. The present mill has been in the ownership of the Thornley family for four generations. The old mill buildings are unique and are surrounded by tidy lawns and flower beds. The mill was originally worked by water but is now turbine driven.

Nearby is the small town of Lymm. Although the building of the Bridgewater Canal and the railway brought trade to the town in the 18th century it remains pleasantly rural with agriculture as its main occupation. The Romans gave the place its name, when they settled there, from their word 'limes' meaning the limits of their territory. They found good building stone and used it in the construction of their camps at Manchester and Chester. In the Domesday Book the village was known as Lime, and from Norman times the manorial rights were in the hands of the Lymme family who, after the Norman fashion, had taken

*Heatley Mill*

*Lymm Cross*

its name from the place. Gilbert de Limme was living at Lymm Hall in the reign of King John, and a family of that name lived there until 1342. The house was rebuilt in the reign of Elizabeth I, and in the mid 19th century it stood within the remains of a moat on a hill not far from Lymm Cross. The house is now a collection of flats.

Lymm Cross is one of the finest in the country. The steps were cut from solid rock for more than half its height – worn by successive generations of children playing on them, they were restored by public donations to commemorate the Diamond Jubilee of Queen Victoria. The old stocks are adjoining, and the structure is in the centre of the old market place. There is a legend that Saint Paul may have preached from the Cross but there is no confirmation of this, and the present cross is probably only 17th century.

A writer in 1673 mentions a church existing at Lymm before the Norman conquest. Church registers go back to 1569. A carved head inserted in the south wall of the church was dug from the foundations of a previous church on the site. The present church was rebuilt and enlarged in 1851. The tower contains a clock and eight bells, the tenor bell being the heaviest in Cheshire apart from one at Chester Cathedral. Rushbearing – carrying the rushes to act as carpets in church – was formerly a great annual festival in August, but this custom has been discontinued. In the days of the stage coaches from Liverpool to Manchester, they travelled through Lymm by way of the

*Mill stones at Heatley Mill.*

41

*The village pump, Warburton.*

*St. Werburgh's, Warburton, one of the oldest surviving timber frame churches in England.*

*Lymm Dam*

steep Eagle Brow, round the Cross, up Church Green and on past the church. To avoid this dangerous twisting route a dam was built about the time of the Crimean War, across the long ravine which crosses the parish, and a main road was built over it. A deep lake was thus formed leaving the church on wooded sloping banks. The walk on the other side of the dam is called 'the Bongs' (a local corruption of the word 'banks').

I returned to the final section of the Bollin one sharp September afternoon. I went along with a friend to see if we could find the end of the river. I knew that the last few miles from the mill ran through privately-owned land and that Bollin Point, where the river actually enters the Manchester Ship Canal, was on the farmland of Reddish Hall, a building constructed in old mellow red brick, and so it had been necessary to obtain the prior consent of the owner. We set off across the fields on a path alongside the river and met a farmhand on a combine harvester, cutting the last of the summer wheat. In the distance above the waving corn it was odd to see the decks and funnels of large ships as they sailed along the canal.

By the time we reached Bollin Point, which is indicated by a large wedge-shaped stone on the right-hand side of the river bank, where the river enters the canal at

right angles to it, the ships had passed on their different ways. This was irritating as I particularly wished to film the ships at close quarters. We waited – perhaps another forty-five minutes getting colder by the minute in the early evening breeze – peering either way for further maritime activity. Our patience was rewarded – several ships came – one a Russian vessel, and we felt our exploration had indeed been well worthwhile.

Just out of view beyond the canal is Rixton Old Hall where successive Lords of the Manor, named Alan de Rixton, lived from 1200 to 1384. In December 1745 the Duke of Cumberland crossed the ferry, which then existed near this point, in pursuit of the Young Pretender.

It is strange to think that the small stream which begins in the region of Tegg's Nose and the Macclesfield Forest and ends thirty miles further on when it joins the Manchester Ship Canal has babbled, spurted and rushed on its way for hundreds of years. Even at its end it is not a great waterway and yet the water has been used to baptise early Christians and cleanse lepers; powered mills for making cotton goods, corn, silk and for sawing wood; as well as providing recreation for thousands whose interests lie in walking, hunting, fishing, sailing and studying botany and ornithology.